MIGHT IS RIGHT

> BEHIND ALL Kings and Presidents, all Govern-
> ment and Law,
> Are army corps and cannoneers to hold the world
> in awe:
> For Might is Right when empires sink in storms of
> steel and flame.
> And it is right when weakling breeds are hunted
> down like game.   —From "Might is Right."

(Previous Page) Detail from the front page title banner of *The Lumberjack*.

(Above) Hall excerpts from the book *Might is Right* as a space-filler in *The Voice of the People*, Vol. 3 No. 10 (March 5, 1914).

Might Is Right: The Rebel Poetry of Covington Hall and His Satanic Lumberjacks, Bombastic & Blasphemic Poetry from a Forgotten Labor Movement
Edited and Introduced by Kevin I. Slaughter.
Revised and Expanded Second Edition.

The first edition was titled *Covington Hall's Satanic Lumberjacks and Southron Rebels*. It was published as a limited edition booklet in 2019.

Published by Underworld Amusements & Union of Egoists.
ISBN: 978-1-943687-14-5, February 2024

More information:
www.UnionOfEgoists.com
www.UnderworldAmusements.com

Stand Alone SA1282

Published as part of the Stand Alone series by the Union of Egoists. Stand Alone is mixed medium and format journal produced at irregular intervals. The focus is Egoism and the individuals associated with it.

Contents

Covington Hall 5
   by Kevin I. Slaughter
The Prophet's Curse 6
When There Isn't Any Money . 6
Ita Est 6
   by Ragnar Redbeard
The "100 Percents" 10
Might is Right 11
Our Father's Way 12
A 1945 Letter to Agnes Inglis . 17
Covington Hall 12
   by Justus Ebert
Rebellion 20
Lucifer, Light-Bearer! 25
Us, the Hoboes 26
The Madman's Boast 27
Forged in Hell 27
   by Israel Zangwill
Mary, the Mother of Christ . 28
What is the I. W. W.? 28
   (Unsigned)
I'd Like to Be a Savage 29
God Said 29
In the Holy Name of Trade . . . 30
Arise 30
Lucifer, the Morning Star . . . 31
Necessity 31
Thank God! 32
   by Harry Kemp
That's Different 32
   by Loring Roper
We Must 33
I, The Soul of Labor 34
I, The Soul 35
Barbarica 36
   by Jim Seymour
Their Gods 37
The Bearers of the Light 38
   by Henry M. Tichenor
Hear! 38
   by Omar
A Prayer to Lucifer 39
Onward Christian Soldiers . . 40
   by Wm. Lloyd Garrison
The Honest Burglar 41
   by Rev. M.A. Smith
A Conjuration 41
Failure 42
A Nightmare's Nest 43
What Lucifer Wrote 43
   by Kaufman
Ye "Respectables" 44
I, The Kept Press 45
Our Boy-Heart 45
   by Voc, the Barbarian
People Will Talk 46
   (Unsigned)
War 47
   by Adolf Wolff
Might is Right (*variant*) 47
Our Primer of Celebrities . . . 48
   (Unsigned)
Offensive Neatness 48
How Much Came True? 49
   by Wilby Heard
The Hobo's Boast 50
Fodder for Cannon 50
   by Katherine Lee Bates
A Rebel's Dream 51
   by Cash M. Stevens
The Curious Christians 52
A Hymn to Hate 53
The Prophet's Curse 53
Confessions 54
O glowing Land of Dixie 55
The Strike 55
The Sons of the Serpent 56
A Prayer to Thor 56
Bibliography 57

A gathering of young males, recognized as "unemployed", in New York City. They are proudly displaying copies of *The Voice of the People*. The edition presented in the middle of the photograph is Vol. 3 No. 8 (Feb. 19, 1914). Every issue of *The Voice of the People* showcases the phrase "Might is Right" prominently. Photo courtesy of the Library of Congress.

Covington Hall:
Wobbly and Redbeardian

Kevin I. Slaughter

Covington Hall (1871-1952) was a poet, teacher, and polemicist most closely associated with the Industrial Workers of the World (Wobblies). This Chicago-based labor union formed in 1905 out of some of the more radical figures of the movement, positioning itself against both commumism and capitalism. Hall was active in the Labor movement for decades and his life and work and his biography has subsequently been kept alive largely by a single academic.

Covington Hall

Born into a wealthy Southern family in 1871, it was just after the turn of the century that Hall had begun engaging in radical politics. He worked on a number of journals and made a name for himself as being more tough and outspoken than even those in the socialist circles.

Covington Hall edited a string of journals over a short period of time that are used as primary source material for this collection. First it was *The Lumberjack*, begun in 1913 during a labor strike by the Brotherhood of Timber Workers in Louisiana. The journal took on a new name that year, *The Voice of the People,* and moved its headquarters to New Orleans. The last few issues were published out of Portland, OR but it folded in late 1914.

It is noted by modern writers that the papers *The Lumberjack* and *The Voice of the People* feaured the Wobbly motto "An Injury to One is an Injury to All", but they *also* contained, from the *first* issue to the *last*, the bold proclamation: "MIGHT IS RIGHT." It is in this detail that it is revealed that Covington Hall was *the greatest proponent* of that infamous social-Darwinist book during the lifetime of its author. *Might is Right* was a cornerstone of his own propaganda efforts during this time and it clearly had a profound influence on his own poetry and prose.

From 1916-1917, Hall published the journal *Rebellion: Made Up of Dreams and Dynamite*. This latter publication featured quotes from Nietzsche, and promoted his new poetry collection *Songs of Love and Rebellion.* It was offered for sale alongside *Might is Right,* Paine's *The Age of Reason,* and Paul Lafargue's *Right to Be Lazy,* among other books.

When There Isn't Any Money

BY COVAMI

When there isn't any money
There isn't any honey
On the battercakes and bread;
And tho the sun is shining
One cannot help repining
And a-wishin' one were dead.

Nor can we help implying
That the Experts all are lying
'Bout "prosperity is here!"
For when we're feeling hollow
It is tough to have to swallow
All this cheerio and cheer.

It is well for those who're eating
To advise us to quit bleating
For the bacon, beer and greens;
But I doubt they'd pep-talk, sonny,
If there wasn't any money
In the bottom of their jeans

Moral

If you want to go to eating,
Can the grouching and the bleating,
And go organize the crew!
For we'll face but stormy weather
Until we get together
In the O. B. U.!

The Prophet's Curse

The Prophet-soul can never rest:
It cannot see, What is, is best;
By a strange demon 'tis possesst—
It has a conscience in its breast.

—COVAMI

ITA EST

Stars and suns may perish,
Empires wax and wane,
But the law of struggle
Eternal shall remain.

Ragnar Redbeard.

The cover and page eight from *The One Big Union Monthly* Vol. 2 No. 1 (January, 1938). This magazine published by the I.W.W. features two poems by Covington Hall, writing under his penname Covami, and one by Arthur Desmond writing as Ragnar Redbeard. Of note is the fact Arthur Desmond died in 1927, just over a decade before the poem was published here, showing a continued support of his work after death.

ΔΔΔ

In his 1948 autobiography *Wobbly: The Rough-and-Tumble Story of an American Radical*, Ralph Chaplin recalled that Redbeard's book was quite well known amont labor agitators:

> One day [prison guard Captain Eddy] found a copy of *Might Makes Right* [sic] in our cell. He picked it up with a grimace. "Is this a Wobbly book?" The question was directed at Dan Buckley, who explained that it had been written a quarter of a century previously by one "Ragnar Redbeard," a diminutive, repressed Near North Side philosopher with delusions of grandeur. "Well, I've noticed a lot of Wobblies reading the damn thing. Let me have it."

Hall's book *Songs of Love and Rebellion* features a poem titled "Might is Right." It is not plagiarism as much as an homage to Redbeard's own poem "The Logic of To-Day." Taking the form and style of Redbeard's poem, he overlays his own themes to make it relavent to Labor's struggles.

As would be expected from a radical poet influenced by Ragnar Redbeard, Hall's writing is often mix of bombastic, violent, anti-religious, and often Satanic themes, with multiple poems explicitly devoted to Lucifer.

Songs of Love and Rebellion was sold directly by the "Satanic Socialist" Henry M. Tichenor from his journal *The Melting Pot*, and the same with the Communist Party journal *The Masses*. The San Francisco anarchist journal *The Blast* advertised it for sale alongside Max Stirner's *The Ego and His Own*, the works of Emma Goldman, Margaret Sanger, Voltairine de Cleyre and Peter Kropotkin. Arthur Desmond, alias "Ragnar Redbeard" and "Richard Thurland", sold Hall's poetry book through his own Thurland and Thurland mail order book outfit.

Hall's poetry would find its way into journals for various tradesmen. Examples include the *The Tailor: Official Organ of the Journeymen Tailors' National Union*, *The Railroad Telegrapher*, *Freight-handler's and Railway Clerk's Journal*, or *Miner's Magazine: The Official Organ of Western Federation of Miners*. I've included a contemporary appreciation of his work from the letters section of *The Industrial Worker*.

While Covington Hall might have been a fringe figure for society at large, we see he was part of the main stable of radical writers of his day, and his promotion of Redbeard among the socialists, anarchists and working men conveys one aspect about how the forgotten history of *Might is Right* is dynamic, surprising, *and probably intentional.*

ΔΔΔ

In 1999 Charles H. Kerr Publishing Company published a volume containing Hall's memoirs and a small collection of writings pulled from journals. The book, titled *Labor Struggles in the Deep South & Other*

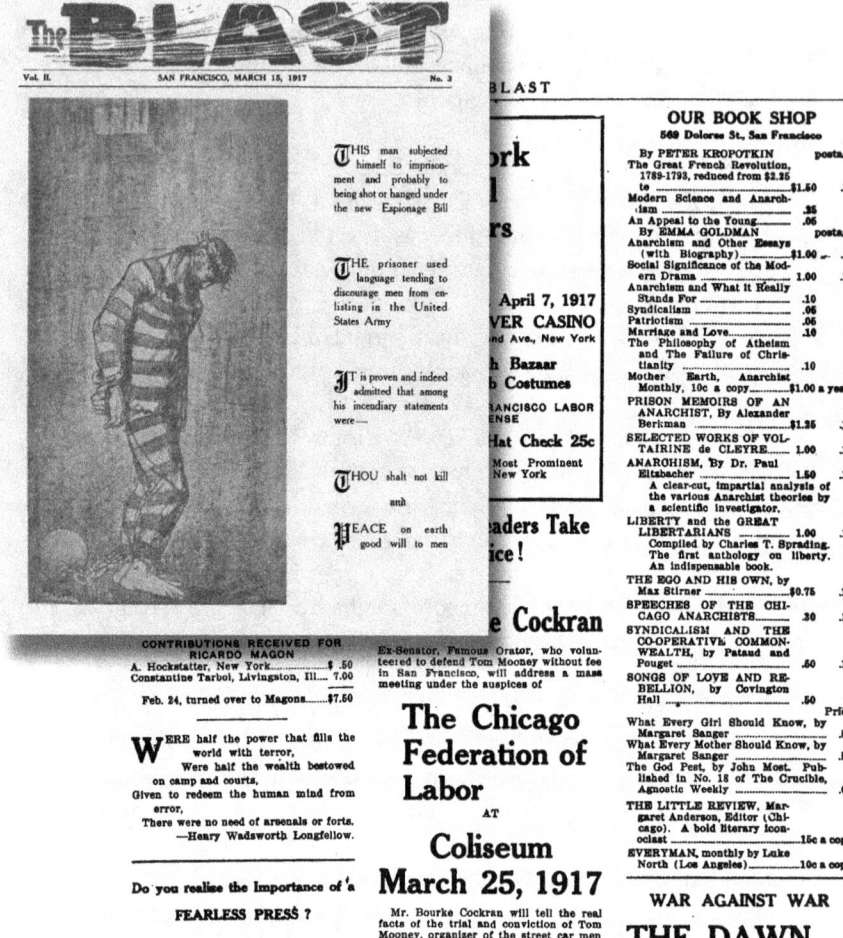

Hall's book was offered for sale by the San Francisco anarchist periodical *The Blast*, alongside Max Stirner's *The Ego and His Own* and Margaret Sanger's works.

Writings, is the single best source for information about Hall's life. The well researched introduction details how the manuscript, completed in 1951, became "lost" in a web of university requests and intellectual property limbo. Curiously neither the book *Might is Right* nor its author Ragnar Redbeard are mentioned.

I could make sense of Hall himself leaving this bit out if he regretted championing the work for so long. *Might is Right* rails against every "sacred" thing, including Labor. But that the introduction of *Labor Stuggles* makes *no mention of it at all* seems a far more puzzling exclusion. The author, an activist professor named David R. Roediger, was seemingly the sole champion of Covington Hall for decades, though not without criticism and qualification. In examining three major pieces by Roedinger on Covington Hall, *not once* do I find Ragnar Redbeard or the book *Might is Right* mentioned. A significant 1992 article on Hall by Donald Winters, from *Labor's Heritage* journal, likewise neglects to acknowledge Redbeard in any way. More books by academics fall into the same pattern.

Redbeard scholarship over the last 127 years has been thin and largely ignored, when it wasn't myopic or merely defamatory. A few academics and independent writers persisted but the information never seemingly spread to the places *academics* actually seem to look, so some of this ignorance is understandable. But still, by 2003, when Jeffory A. Clymer published *America's Culture of Terrorism,* in an eleven page discussion of Covington Hall, not once is the name Ragnar Redbeard mentioned or even the title *or* phrase "Might is Right" used!

That is *too much* for *all* to be a mere coincidence. Hall made sure the phrase was the *first thing* a reader saw when picking up a copy of *The Lumberjack* in 1913, and dedicated a poem to the book. That poem was influential enough that is is included in many editions of *The Little Red Songbook,* the iconic and official I.W.W. songbook. Comrades who gathered to sing in solidarity would see Hall/Redbeard's words if they happened to hold a Twenty-first edition printed in 1925 until at least the thirty-first edition from 1964. It was recently included in the compilation titled *The Big Red Songbook,* with the description prefacing the poem there makes reference to *Labor Struggles* but, again, no mention of the *explicit inspiratation* for the song. That is *too much* to be a *mere coincidence.*

I am appreciative of David R. Roediger's work nonetheless, and surely I show my own bias and place too much emphasis, in reaction, as the publisher and editor of *Might is Right: The Authoritative Edition.* I found Hall via Redbeard, and marvel at the idea that thousands of people, beginning over a hundred years ago, also have found Redbeard via Hall, and therefore from the context of Labor and Union organizing.

∆∆∆

The collection that follows consists of poems largely culled from his

THE "100 PERCENTS"

By Covami

They went to war—on platforms;
   They heard the boom—of bands;
They fought—for army contracts;
   They marched—on public lands.

Thus, thus through the ages
   They have skirted round the fray,
Urging boys to rape and slaughter
   That their guileful breed might prey;
Till the Earth is one vast shambles,
   Whence they came up from their marts
With Christ upon their lech'rous lips
   With murder in their hearts.

L'Envoi

"Put no hope in Princes",
   Is a saying old and true;
"Put no trust in 'Patriots' ",
   Translateth it anew;
Their one and only object
   Is the masses to betray,
"A curse is on their cankered brains,
   Their very bones decay!"

The "Covami" poem, titled "The "100 Percents"", as published in the *Industrial Democrat* (Leesville, Louisiana) in the October 24, 1935 issue. The "L'Envoi", a sort of postscript added to the end of a poem, makes explicit quotation of the poem "The Logic of To-Day", published in Ragnar Redbeard's *Might is Right*. Of note is the fact that this was printed over two decades since the first issue of *The Lumberjack*, showing a sustained appreciation for the "Redbeard Philosophy" as lumberjack anarchist James "Second Jesus" Rowan refers to it.

journals *The Lumberjack*, *The Voice of the People* and *Rebellion*, all from a short span of a few years between 1913 and 1917. When the source journal noted any piece was reprinted from elsewhere, I have mentioned that in a footnote. When I have drawn from a different source, I have footnoted that. Nearly all of the poems are by Covington, but I have included other writers as well, when their work lent itself to themes developed in the collection. Because Hall sometimes wrote in "voices" depending on the pen name, I've decided to credit authorship to whatever name was listed in the source.

Prior to the completion of *Labor Struggles*, David R. Roediger edited and introduced a collection of poetry titled *Dreams & Dynamite*, published in 1985 by Kerr. This collection has many pieces it didn't, and vice versa.

By the time Hall's last collection of poetry was published in 1946, a few years before his death, it appears he'd shed much of his Satanic & Redbeardian posturing, and so therefore there is quite little overlap between the present collection and his *Battle Hymns of Toil*. There are at least two incredibly rare volumes of Hall's work that I have not been able to inspect.

△△△

My comrade Trevor Blake has culled through Hall's journals in his own studies and I have benefitted directly by his research in the creation of this collection. I credit him here with having made my work far better and easier.

MIGHT IS RIGHT

Might was right when Christ was hanged
  Beside the Jordan's foam;
Might was right when Gracchus bled,
  Upon the stones of Rome;
And might was right when Danton fell,
  When Emmet passed away—
"'Tis the logic of the ancient world,
  And the gospel of today."

Might was right when Spartacus
  Went down in seas of blood,
And when the Commune perished
  In the self-same crimson flood;
And might was right at Cripple Creek,
  At Homestead, Grabow—yea!
"'Tis the logic of the ancient world,
  And the gospel of today."

(cont.)

OUR FATHERS' WAY

(By Covington Hall)

Or right or wrong, like men they fought,
Like men they lived, like men they wrought,
Like men they died—like men!—like men!—
How changed the breed twixt now and then!

Then, blow for blow and woe for woe,
They brooked no insults from the foe;
And side by side, and man to man,
They rode together in the Clan.

They swore to swear to truth or lie,
To win together or to die;
So, come what would, no man was loth,
For by their blood they swore this oath.

They laughed to scorn the gunmen's might,
And forayed thru the fog-hung night;
From mountain crag and swampy dell
Like sheeted ghosts upon them fell.

They had no use for currish tricks,
The sophistries of politics;
Of Plundercrats they had no awe,
No ermined crook to them was law.

• • • • • • • •

The wood was thick—the moon was bright—
The Clansmen knew that might was right.

The cover and page twenty-two from *The Eagle and the Serpent* Vol. 18 No. 4 (July 1915). This magazine was published by Arthur Desmond during a period where he used the name "Richard Thurland," one of dozens of aliases he used during his life. Though it has a high volume number, it is plausible that only one issue was ever published under this name. Desmond prints two of Hall's poems and offers Hall's book *Poems of Love and Rebellion* for sale.

Might was right when Parsons died.
　　When Ferrer followed him,
When Cole's young life was beaten out
　　In Spokane's dungeons grim;
And might was right when Pettibone
　　Went stagg'ring down death's way—
"'Tis the logic of the ancient world.
　　And the gospel of today."

Might is right when Morgan builds
　　A hell 'round every hearth;
Might is right when Kirby starves
　　His peons off the earth;
And might was right when Deitz became
　　Wolfe Weyerhauser's prey—
"'Tis the logic of the ancient world.
　　And the gospel of today."

Might is right when children die
　　By thousands in the mills,
When jeweled hands reach down and take
　　The gold their blood distills;
And might is right when maidens give
　　Their love-dreams up for pay—
"'Tis the logic of the ancient world,
　　And the gospel of today."

Might was, it is, it e'er will be.
　　The one and only right;
And so, hosts of toil, awaken!
　　O workingmen, unite!
Unite! Unite! For might is right—
　　'Tis freedom's only way—
"'Tis the logic of the ancient world,
　　And the gospel of today."

A 1945 letter to Agnes Inglis of the Joseph A. Labadie Collection.

N.O.15, LA.[1]
-4-10-45-

Miss Agnes Inglis,
  Ann Arbor, Mich.

Dear Friend:-

Your letter of 5th, with enclosures, reached me yesterday, and I know not how to thank you for all the trouble you are going to aid us in our history. I do, tho. I cannot judge, however, what issue of the papers may be of use by the numbers you list; so, it is making you do useless work to send me the lists, tho I greatly appreciate your doing so.

Answering your queries seratim: the poem, "Might is Right", was first written by Ragnar Redbeard. The two versions of mine were written at later dates, the last being revised to meet changed social conditions, as many of my poems have been, notable "The Way of Kings, Crowned and Uncrowned". I do not know who "Ragnar Redbeard" really was.[2] Thurland would never reveal his identity. We, however, suspected he was himself the author. Arthur Desmond, the great Australian poet and agitator, was once credited with the book, "Might Is Right; or The Survival of the Fittest", in which the poem first appeared. I have heard that, on the Pacific Coast, I was given credit, if credit it be, of writing the book; but I did not. My belief is that Thurland was the author. He usually "talked strong" but was careful not to sign his name to any "raw stuph". A young Swiss engineer who once visited New Orleans, said the book was "a rehash in raw American of the writings of Max Stirner, Nietzsche, and other European writers of doom"; that there was nothing really original about it. The book, according to Thurland, was first

---

1   Letters between Covington Hall and Agnes Inglis provided by the Joseph A. Labadie Special Collection at the University of Michigan. I have only lightly edited his writing.
2   It is unknowable if this is a true statement. While Arthur Desmond never fully concealed his identity as Redbeard in Australia and New Zealand, he was so successful in the United States that it wasn't known in the US until British egoist historian Sidney E. Parker made a definitive connection in 1985. It was in the "letters column" of the New York gay anarcist journal *The Storm*, published by Mark A. Sullivan, the issue following his own essay that became the introduction to the Loompanics Unlimited edition of *Might is Right*. Unfortunately the journal was obscure and Parker's clarity would not be picked up by subsequent writers. It would be after the turn of the 21st century before American Redbeard scholars would catch on.

published in London in 1896 and circulated privately to a few.[3] If it was then first published, it contains a remarkably prophesy, viz: That the world on the eve of a catastrophic war. "Peace, peace, peace, you talk peace?" says Redbeard, "With all Europe a powder magazine and a maniac standing in the middle of it waving a flamin torch! Peace? Bah!" Many have asked me why I circulated the book. I did so to stir up the Southern people and get them over their inferiority complex as a conquered people, I told them.

(...)[4]

> I remain,
> Gratefully yours,
> Covington Hall

P.S... I have written under the following pen names: Covington Ami, Covami, Ole Smoke, W.C.Ould, or, simply, Covington, and Notgnivoc The Barbarian. This I did so that my name might not appear too often in any paper.

---

[3] A short manuscript edition existed in 1896, but textual evidence reveals that the full book, as we know it today, was not published until late 1897. More details are provided in *Might is Right: The Authoritative Edition* (Baltimore: Underworld Amusements, 2019).
[4] I have not transcribed the middle portion of the letter, dealing with other inquiries not pertinent to this collection.

Illustration found in *The Voice of the People* Vol. 3 No. 11 (March 12, 1914). New Orleans, LA. This illustration was recalled by Hall in his book *Labor Struggles in the Deep South* on pg. 173.

YE POET-EDITOR OF REBELLION AS SEEN BY YE REBEL CARTOONIST, B. W. LAUDERDALE.

Illustration from *Rebellion: Made up of Dreams and Dynamite*
Vol. I No. 7 (January, 1916). New Orleans, LA.

Covington Hall: An Appreciation of His Works As the Poet of the Revolution.

Justus Ebert[5]

There is a great objection in certain quarters to the praise of individuals in our ranks. We may sing the praises of, and quote, Nietszche, we may be saturated with his philosophy, but we must have no Nietszche among us. We are democrats, with the many inconsistencies and incongruities peculiar to a democracy; in fact, we are a democracy because of them, and not in spite of them. So, your leave, we will now proceed to praise one among us, who is deserving of praise; not because we would exalt the superman, but because we consider certain pronounced personifications of tendencies within the revolutionary movement worthy of notice at all times. Covington Hall is one of those personifications. He personifies the poetic spirit of the revolution better than any man in the movement today, barring none.

To define Covington Hall is difficult. In some quarters he is considered mad. He should not feel hurt on that account. Madness is the gift of poets. And we often think of the lines of the old English dramatist, Michael Drayton, when we think of Covington Hall:

> "Next Marlowe, bathed in the Thespian springs
> Had in him those brave translunary things
> That the first poets had: his raptures were
> All air and fire, which made his verses clear;
> For that fine madness still he did retain
> Which rightly should possess a poet's brain."

The "fine madness" of Marlowe has Covington Hall. He has those "brave translunary things" of the "first poets; the raptures" that are "all air and fire"— the fire, not of the flamboyant mouther, but of the Hebraic prophet of old.

Perhaps, "gentle reader," you don't believe this, Perhaps you think the reviewer is afflicted with a madness that is neither fire nor poetic; he's simply "nutty." Turn then to any of Covington Hall's current poetry. Turn to his poem in the May Day issue of the *Industrial Worker*:

---

5   *The Industrial Worker*, Vol 5 No 8 (May 15, 1913).

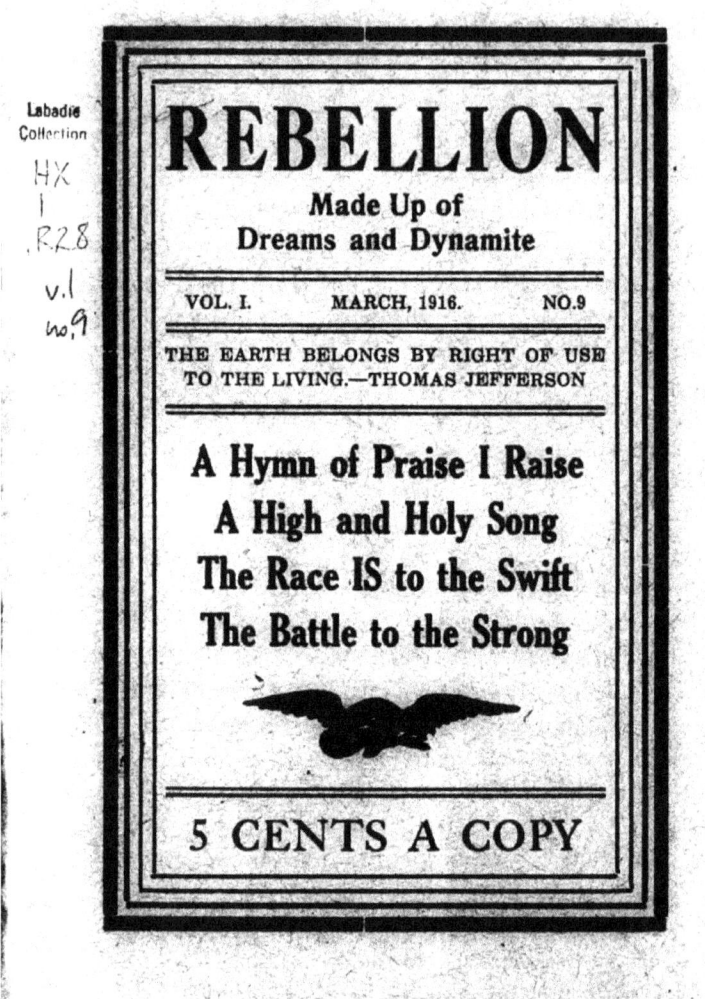

The cover of *Rebellion: Made up of Dreams and Dynamite* Vol. 1 No. 9 (March 1916), published in New Orleans, LA. The exact quote on the cover was used by Arthur Desmond in advertisements for *Might is Right*. It is an inversion of Ecclesiates 9:11 and was popular phrase in a post-Darwinian world. Jack London's titular character from *Martin Eden* (1909) says "I believe the race is to the swift, the battle to the strong. Such is the lesson I have learned from biology, or at least think I have learned." In the quote as presented, it seems Desmond has paraphrased the first stanza of Scottish poet John Davidson's "War Song," published in 1890: "In anguish we uplift | A new unhallowed song: | The race is to the swift; | The battle to the strong." Cover digitized from microfilm of an item in the Joseph A. Labadie Special Collection at the University of Michigan.

"The Ways of Kings, Crowned and Uncrowned." What power is there! True poetic power, united with the historical culture of the scholar, and the fiery teal of the revolutionist, it is not difficult to feel the strength of this magnificent poem, nor to respond to its intellectual and moral stimuli. Consider the beauty of these six lines taken from this superb work:

> Where are India's mighty princes? Where the Babylonian kings?
> Tell me, ye who kneel in worship at the shrine of earthly things.
> Proud ye are, and will not answer—ye are swelled with folly vast;
> Neither will ye heed the lesson that is taught in ages past.
> Like the scribes of ancient Judah ye depend on Roman might.
> But the buried Christ is risen and the faith still lives to-night.

Who can read the world-history of civilization embodied in these lines without both feeling and realizing the triumph of the revolutionary ideal in the progress of the race? These lines are prophetic and recall Lowell's great poem of the Civil War, "The Crisis." The whole of Covington Hall's poem ranks with Lowell's, if not above it!

It is almost a decade since the writer was first attracted to Covington Hall's works. He soon became aware that Hall was a dialectician of no mean calibre; and like most dialecticians of that character, he has a keen satiric wit and the deft touch of humorous characterization.

For example, take another one of Hall's current poems, "Behold!" in the May Day issue of *The Lumberjack*, which he edits so well us to earn the hatred of the Southern Lumber Trust. Let us begin with the first verse:

> Behold Bob Hunter tear along,
> A Moon Cheeld lost In senseless song;
> A mushy, mouthy sort of cuss.
> An intellectual blunderbuss!

In the language of the day, "can you beat it" as a characterization of Hunter? That quatrain has a slam-bang style, but it is true to life. Here's another verse, better yet—

> Behold Os. Ameringer soak
> The One Big Union with a joke!
> A Umorist gone dippy drunk,
> Looned by his own bullcon and bunk!

Next time Ameringer tries to "soak, the One Big Union with a Joke," he wants to make sure Hall is not around to turn the poke against him. Note the use of the vernacular by Hall, as contrasted with the classical language used in the first poem, quoted in this article. This is a testimonial of his assimilative and adaptive qualities, which will be found In all good poets.

Covington Hall is as keen and at satiric a poet as ever scuttled the opposition. But it is not to be believed that he is cynical or calloused to the tender, emotional side of life. We recall that, a few years ago, there died in New Orleans a Socialist woman, whose good deeds won the praise of our poet in a memorial poem that was impressive and touching, not only as an appreciation of her noble character, but as a reflection of his own. We have lost that poem, in the hurly-burly of life. But we recollect it as one of the most exquisite things Covington Hall had ever penned.

Right here we wish to express the hope that Covington Hall will follow the good example of his fellow-poet-in-the-revolution, Giovannitti; and publish his poems in one splendid volume. They would then be preserved, where now they are lost, to us.[6]

We would like to quote Hall's poem, "The World Builders," which he had "dedicated to Fellow Workers Fredonia Steventon and Ruby Idom and all the warrior women of the Working South." But space forbids. It will be found in the May Day issue of *The Lumberjack*, to which every reader of this should subscribe and thus help our good Southern poet in his noble work for the revolution.

We will close with a poem that will speak more eloquently for itself than can any words of ours:

REBELLION

Rebellion comes, hope's sacred fire,
    To Freedom's son from Freedom's sire;
A soul-breath swordsmen cannot kill,
    Nor gold, nor cross, nor rifle still.

With Lucifer it marched on God
    And broke Jehovah's scourging rod:
It stood with Christ in Pilate's hall
    And doomed the Caesars to their fall.

---

[6] After the letter was written, and before the present volume, multiple collections of poetry have been printed. We have produced a bibliography of Hall's work at the end of this volume.

It sent Gautama on his quest,
>Him Asia calls her light and blest;
With Quetzalcoatl, long ago,
>It stirred the heart of Mexico.

With Moses it for freedom sought;
>With wild Mahomet, too, it fought;
It gave Zoroaster all his fame,
>Confucius his deathless name.

With Cromwell's legions, grim and cold.
>It trampled on the statutes old;
With Voltaire, Marat and St. Just,
>It raged 'till Europe rose from dust.

It called Abe Lincoln from the plains,
>Set Marx and Ferrer breaking chains,
And hovered o'er the Commune when
>It fired the souls of workingmen.

'Tis that which stirs the race today—
>'Tis that which makes truth's lightnings play—
'Tis Revolution in its birth—
>The soul of Freedom—the light of earth—
>>**REBELLION!**

REBELLION
AND
SONGS OF LOVE AND REBELLION
ON SALE AT:

Staub's Newsstand, Common, near Carondelet, City.

Holle's Newsstand, 613 Camp, City.

Radical Book Shop, 817 1-2 N. Clark Street, Chicago, Ill.

M. Aldeman's Book ,Shop, 291 Tremont street, Boston, Mass.

Book Omnorium, 1350 Fillmore street, San Francisco, Cal.

Advertisement for his journal *Rebellion* and book *Songs of Love and Rebellion*, noting various places it is for sale, including The Radical Book Shop of Chicago, a favorite hangout for Wobblies.

The front page of *The Lumberjack* Vol. I No. I (January, 1913) Alexandria, LA. The statement "MIGHT IS RIGHT" are the first words on it.

The Rebel Poetry of Covington Hall and His Satanic Lumberjacks

Illustration from the cover of *The Voice of the People* [57] *Vol. III No. 6 (February 5th, 1914)*.

LUCIFER, LIGHT-BEARER![7]

Lucifer, Light-Bearer! what a fight is that we made
Since, in hate of thought, they drove us from the Eden-shade;
Out, away from heaven, to, the lonely wastes of hell—
But democracy is winning, and the fight goes well!

What tho we have faltered when the last star cease to shine?—
Ever have we met the priesthoods on the battle-line!
Ever and forever thru the long, long night we've fought,
Hungered, naked, bleeding, for the liberty of thought.

Lucifer, Light-Bearer! how they hate us, how they hate us!
But our star at last is shining over every state!
Everywhere the thrones are crumbling into blackened dust;
And the fruit of knowledge ripens into love and trust.

Backward we are driving, out into the deserts dim,
Backward, from the tree of life, the jealous seraphim;
Backward, from the garden-earth their eunuchs did distress—
And the Man grows greater as the Kings grow less and less.

Lucifer, Light-Bearer! we whose blood runs red within,
By gods hated as the wild democracy of sin;
We the ever-hunted, we the vagrants of the skies,
We still war for freedom, still the slavish we despise!

We still stand unconquered, in rebellion still today,
After all the bitter ages holding still our sway;
Warring, now as ever, for the right to speak our thought,
Without asking from Authority consent for aught!

---

[7] *The Lumberjack*, Vol. 1 No. 3 (Jan. 23, 1913).

US, THE HOBOES[8]

We shall laugh to scorn your power that now holds the world in awe,
We shall trample on your customs and shall spit upon your law;
We shall come up from life's desert to your burdened banquet hall,
We shall turn your wine to wormwood, your honey into gall.

We shall go where wail the children, where, from your race-killing mills,
Flows a bloody stream of profit to your cursed, insatiate tills;
We shall tear from your drivers, in our shamed and angered pride,
With the fury and the fierceness of a fatherhood denied.

We shall set our sisters on you, those you trapt into your hells
Where the mother instinct's stifled and no earthly beauty dwells;
We shall call them from the living-death, the death in life you gave,
To sing our class' triumph o'er your cruel system's grave.

We shall strip them of their epaulets, the panderers who fight
Your wars against the workers for a bone on which to bite;
We shall batter down your prisons, we shall see your chain-gangs free,
We shall drive you from the mountainside, the valley, plain and sea.

We shall hunt around the fences where your ox-men sweat and gape
Till they stampede down your stockades in their panic to escape;
We shall steal up thru the darkness, we shall prowl the wood and town,
Till they waken to their power and arise and ride you down.

We shall send the message to them, on a whisper down the night,
We shall cheer as warrior women drive the ox-men to the fight;
We shall use your guile against you, all the cunning you have taught,
All the wisdom of the serpent to attain the ending sought.

We shall come as comes the cyclone,—in the stillness we shall form—
From the calm your terror fashioned we shall hurl on you the storm;
We shall strike when least expected, when you deem toil's rout complete,
And crush you and your hessians 'neath our brogan-shodded feet.

We shall laugh to scorn your power that now holds the world in awe,
We shall trample on your customs, we shall spit upon your law,
We shall outrage all your temples, we shall blaspheme all your gods,—
We shall turn the old world over as the plowman turns the clods!

---

8   *The Voice of the People*, Vol. 2 No 41 (October 16, 1913).

THE MADMAN'S BOAST[9]
(Dedicated to the "Safe and the Sane")

What know you of madness, you whose minds have never gone astray?
You whose souls have never wandered from the path of common clay?
You who know no other kingdom save this sorrow-stricken earth,
Where you wander in the barrens 'neath the curse of mortal birth!

Lo! how dare you call me crazy? You who live down in the plain,
Far beneath the dazzling empire of the man you call insane!
You are the same forever, just a sentient, moving clod,
While to-day I am a mortal and to-morrow I am God!

I who walk this floor of diamonds, with my head among the stars,
While you dream your keepers hold me chained behind your prison bars!
I who hear immortal music, soft, strange raphsodies divine,
Played for me by master demons when the moons of madness shine!

I who range the clouds of evening when the western sun sinks low,
Drunken with undying splendor and afire with the glow!
I who dwell with Love and Laughter, who the face of Joy behold,
And who never yet have worshiped at the cloven feet of Gold!

You! 'tis you who are the madman! You whose eyes are on the ground,
Kneeling with Ahriman's angels, with the gyves of custom bound!
You who never knew the pleasure and who never felt the pain
Of the souls who roam the empire of the man you call insane!

FORGED IN HELL[10]
Israel Zangwill

"To safeguard peace we must prepare for war"—
I know the maxim: it was forged in hell.
This wealth of ships and guns inflames the vulgar
And makes the very war it guards against.
The God of war is now a man of business,
With vested interests.

---

9   *The Lumberjack*, Vol. 1 No. 19 (May 15, 1913).
10   *The Lumberjack*, Vol. 1 No. 20 (May 22, 1913).

MARY, THE MOTHER OF CHRIST[11]

On Golgotha's barren mountain-top two thousand years ago,
Knelt the mother of a convict keeping watch upon his wo;
Guarding, with that other Mary, in the brute mob all alone,
Fearlessly beside the dying, at the great Blasphemer's throne.

Brokenheartedly she murmured o'er and o'er the words of love,
Reaching thru the tragic darkness to the stricken form above;
Seeking with the mother-magic to give comfort to his pain,
Weeping when he cried for mercy to Authority in vain.

In the midst of all the legions, of the law in all its might,
Of the murdrous priesthood jeering, as they've ever jeered the right,
Knelt the mother of the convict, of the outcast hanging there,
Unaffrighted by the clamor, in her beautiful despair.

Far across the weary centuries I seem to see her still,
She the loving and the gentle, on that blackened, blood-wet hill;
Watching, with that other Mary, in the brute mob all alone,
Fearlessly beside the dying, at the great Blasphemer's throne.

WHAT IS THE I. W. W.?[12]
(Unsigned)

The Capitalists won't "recognize" us.
The Anarchists say we are "Socialists."
The Socialists say we are "Syndicalists."
The Syndicalists say we are "Dual Unioinists."
The Dual Unionists, alias the American Separation
    of Labor, say we are "Nihilists."
The priests and preachers say we are "Infidels."
The Infidels say we are "New Religionists."
Uncle Trusty says we are a "Labor Trust."
They all say we are "Social Rebels."
All of them see part of the truth, for the I. W. W.
    is the NEW AGE being born, the embryo of
    INDUSTRIAL DEMOCRACY!

---

11   *The Lumberjack*, Vol. 1 No. 13 (April 3rd, 1913).
12   *The Lumberjack*, Vol. 1 No. 14 (April 10th, 1913).

I'D LIKE TO BE A SAVAGE[13]
Notgnivoc, The Barbarian

I'd like to be a savage fer a little while agen,
En go out in the forests where there ain't business men;
Where I'd never hear the clatter uv their factories and things,
But jest the low, soft buzzin' uv the hummin's crimson wings
The dronin' uv the bumble bees, en ol' bobwhite's luvin' call
To his mate acrost the medders when the leaves begin to fall.

I'd like to be a savage, ur a barefoot boy agen,
A-roamin' thru the clover, where there ain't no business men;
Where the whole derned tribe is strangers, en their dollars en their dimes
Don't never 'sturb the music o' the gurgling water-rhymes;
Where a feller's heart kin nestle close to Mother Natur's breast,
En the orioles en redbirds sing his tired soul to rest.

I'd like to be a savage, en uncivilized agen,
A member uv a nation where there ain't no business men;
Where no wimmen folks ain't driven to the sweatshops every day;
En the children don't do nuthin', 'cept run en romp en play;
Where the dollar ain't ez mitey ez the song the mockin' sings,
En a feller's heart ain't hurted when he stops to think o' things.

GOD SAID[14]

You loco me with praying.
You tire me with bunc;
I am sick of your petitions.
Your priests and preachers punk.
If you want the land, go, take it!
I am wearied of your need:
I have filled the earth with plenty:
Have your brains all run to seed?
Cut out your cry for saviors.
To be murdered in my sight;
Come off your knees, you lobsters.
And learn to think and fight!

---

13 *The Lumberjack*, Vol.1 No. 4 (January 30th, 1913).
14 *The Voice of the People*, Vol. II No. 35 (September 4th, 1913).

IN THE HOLY NAME OF TRADE[15]

Can you tell me, O ye workers, why the money-demon gloats,
Why the rulers never stop yet when ye tear each other's throats?
Can ye tell me, O ye toilers, why the young are stoopt and old,
Why so many work a-hungered when the land is filled with gold?
"Yea! For profit, profit, profit, all these broken hearts are made—
In the holy name of trade!
In the holy name of trade!"

Can ye tell me, kings of commerce, when machines should on them wait,
Why the burden bears the hardest on the weakest in the State?
Can ye tell me, O my masters, why invention's mighty breath
Only fills the sail that hastens with the children on to death?
"Yea! For profit, profit, profit, all these broken hearts are made—
In the holy name of trade!
In the holy name of trade!"

Can ye tell me, laureled statemen, why around so many hearths
Broods a shadow and a terror that is not our mother earth's?
Can ye tell me, O ye teachers, why, with all the wealth we find,
Why the race in sorrow's mothered and the love-sight's going blind?
"Yea! For profit, profit, profit, all these broken hearts are made—
In the holy name of trade!
In the holy name of trade!"

ARISE![16]
Covami

Thou canst not hear the voice clear
Of Freedom with a slave-tuned ear.

With downcast eyes, in kneeling guise,
Thou canst but read the old, old lies.

On suppliant knee thou canst not be
Of truth and justice devotee.

Who never tries, life ever flies
O slaves of slave, arise! arise!

---

15 *The Voice of the People*, Vol. II No. 44 (November 19th, 1914).
16 *Industrial Worker* Vol. XII No. 25 (June 21, 1930).

LUCIFER, THE MORNING STAR[17]

He was the first to face the wrath of priesthoods and of kings;
He was the first to make his mind the judgment-place of things ;
He was the first to question, first to feel the steel of might—
Lucifer, the Morning Star, the splendid and the bright!

Around his shining spirit, lo! the priests of earth have thrown,
A shadow and a terror that belongs to kings alone—
A demon demons made him, crowned him prince of Utmost Night—
Lucifer, the Morning Star, the splendid and the bright!

Through ages upon ages, they have cursed him day on day,
But fearless and unconquered he has held them all at bay;
Forever and forever he has faced them in the fight—
Lucifer, the Morning Star, the splendid and the bright!

Hail to the first of rebels! To the chieftain, strong and brave,
Who sounded first the bugle-call of freedom to the slave!
Who never yet has faltered through time's long and dreary flight—
Lucifer, the Morning Star, the splendid and the bright!

NECESSITY[18]

Dream ye not that ye will conquer in a single day;
For the great world was not fashioned by a child at play.
Backward through the ages gazing, this one lesson see:
Man is but the product of his necessity.
That the *life* we *live* is moulded by the *life* we *lead*;
And the *life* we *lead* is bounded by the things we *need*.

---

17   *The Voice of the People*, Vol. II No. 34 (August 28th, 1913).
18   *The Voice of the People*, Vol. II No. 28 (July 17th, 1913).

THANK GOD![19]
Harry Kemp

Thank God, I'm not a gentleman,
That I feel free to swear and shout,
That I can sometimes lose my head
And not know what I am about.

Thank God, I have no double way
That I can put on like a suit—
One for the women who obey
The Code, one for the Prostitute.

Yes, thank God, I've no little code,
No paltry ethics of a clan,
No proper and well-beaten road—
Thank God, I'm not a gentleman!

THAT'S DIFFERENT[20]
Loring Roper

Come join John Junior's Bible class,
    In Rockefeller's school.
And learn about the pure in heart,
    Likewise the Golden Rule.
To love your neighbor as yourself,
    Nor pass the sinner by,
Unless he dares go out on strike,
    Is John's great pious cry.
He'll tell you of his vice crusade,
    Preach mercy from on high,
But no compassion stirs within
    When miners' children die.
Let's prate of meekness and of love,
    Talk brotherhood of man,
But when a minor dares to strike,
    Why; kill him if you can.

---

19   *The Lumberjack*, Vol. 1 No. 22 (June 5th, 1913).
20   *The Voice of the People*, Vol. II No. 40 (October 22nd, 1914).

WE MUST[21]

From out their gloomy caverns, from their dungeons dank and cold,
The dead men rule the living and eternal empire bold;
Our fathers' bones forever weight our spirit's upward flight,
Their shrouds are held between us and the fullness of the light.

Across our yearning soul-sight, lo; the hand of Pluto rests,
And Javeth's heel still crushes out the flame within our breasts;
The word of Tamerlane and Torquemada still is law,
And cross and sword have power still the world to overawe.

The city by Potomac's chained to London's mouldy shrines,
And over all of London Rome's death-giving luster shines;
And back of Rome is Nineveh; and Semiramis sways,
Her sceptre blights the nations now as in the yesterdays.

The sinful eye of Solomon still casts its evil spell,
And Joseph has the power still to make of earth a hell;
The vampires, Calvin and Loyola, brood on Europe's breast,
The frown of werewolf Cortez falls athwart the glowing West.

Forever and forever, where the ark of freedom stands,
The dead men meet the living with their stern and harsh commands;
Forever and forever, on whatever soil we tread,
The army of the living fronts the army of the dead.

Forever and forever must truth's ever-seeking hosts,
Be ready to give battle to our sires' angry ghosts;
Forever and forever, on our onward upward march,
We must raze our father's tombstones and must break their temple's arch.

---

21   *The Lumberjack* Vol. 1 No. 27 (July 10, 1913).

I, THE SOUL OF LABOR[22]

There is no earthly power strong enough
To bar my way; there is no road so rough
But I will follow to the fartherest goal,
Or, failing, fall unconquered—I, the Soul.

Your class-made creeds, I hate, despise and curse,
For I am that Democracy did nurse;
Like cobwebs I would tear them from my brain
And walk alone the vales of life again.

What tho priest and politician 'round me scream
The lunacy of some fantastic dream?
Think you these gibbering things can blind
The mind unto the vision soul-divined!

Amid the wreck of worldly things I move
Unfettered; my own body does but prove
My independence, for I loathe its lust,
Its crawling and its cringing in the dust.

The all that ever was, it is but ME;
In ME, the end of all that comes, you see;
For I, and I alone, march on with God
Unfearing o'er the unknown, trackless sod.

My fate it is my own to make or mar;
I am my spirit's good and evil star;
And here, or after here, let come what will,
I am and shall be my own master still—
I, THE SOUL OF LABOR!

---

[22] *The Lumberjack*, Vol. 1 No. 23 (June 12th, 1913).

I, THE SOUL[23]

There is no earthly power strong enough
To bar my way; there is no road so rough
But I will follow to the fartherest goal.
Or, failing, fall unconquered—I, the Soul.

Your man-made creeds, I hate, despise and curse,
For I am that Eternal Love did nurse;
Like cobwebs I would tear them from my brain
And walk, alone, the vales of truth again.

What tho your priest and preacher 'round me scream
The lunacy of some fantastic dream;
Think you these gibbering things can blind
The mind unto the vision self-divined!

Amid the wreck of worldly things I move
Unfettered; my own body does but prove
My independence, for I loathe its lust.
Its crawling and its cringing in the dust.

The all that ever was, it is but me;
In me, the end of all that comes, you see;
For I, and I alone, march on with God
Unfearing o'er the unknown, trackless sod.

My fate it is my own to make or mar;
I am my spirit's good and evil star;
And here, or after here, let come what will,
I am and shall be my own master still.

---

[23] This variant was printed in *Rebellion*, with important distinctions.

BARBARICA[24]
Jim Seymour

Within the heart of regions unexplored,
There lies a land where freedom is unknown
The natives are a most unthinking horde
Who fight like beasts o'er gristle, hide and bone;
The short one hates his brother who is tall,
Young Bright-eye loathes the old one who is blind,
And each by all the rest is kept a thrall,
Because he fails to recognize his kind.

Within this land of prejudice and hate,
A king has ruled (as kings forever must)
By fostering dislike of mate for mate,
And teaching all to worship golden lust;
And while the workers quarrel for the hulls
From off the product of their daily task
The king in public places hangs the skulls
Of those who for the grain itself would ask.

Among the cheerless huts where workers dwell,
The hireling agents of the king are seen;
Their fetid breath is like a blast from hell,
To those on whom they choose to vent their spleen;
The toiling widow sinks beneath their blows,
Her babe is lured to death by poisoned milk;
And still a smile of sing contentment glows,
On all the faces of their bastard ilk.

And while at home this tragedy is played,
Another is enacted at the mill;
The widow's elder children, boy and maid,
Are driven to their work till rendered ill;
In hunger and fatigue they sweat and strain,
Until the boy falls dying to the floor;
And then the girl, despite her grief and pain,
To pay for burial rites must work the more.

In after weeks, the while this little girl,
Alone and homeless, suffers at the mill,

---

24   *The Voice of the People*, Vol. II No. 30 (July 31st, 1913).

The king and court enjoy the social whirl
Within the royal mansion on the hill;
The music plays, the dance is gayly tript,
Then at the lanquet board the gathering rests,
Where flesh that from the workgirl's bones was stript,
Is served on golden platters to the guests.

'Twere best perhaps that I should tell no more
About the savage customs of the land,
For after all 'tis on some distant shore
And foreign ways are hard to understand;
This awful country that to-night I see,
Is farther many billion times than Mars;
So let us praise "America the Free,"
And think no more of life beyond the stars.

THEIR GODS[25]

If God is that which blesses, benefits the worshipper, then it must be that:

The Landlord's God is RENT.
The Banker's God is INTEREST.
The Capitalist's God is PROFIT.
The Politician's God is GRAFT.
The Judge's God is PRECEDENT.
The Clergyman's God is CREDULITY.
The Soldier's God is LOOT.
The Gunman's God is PANTHER JUICE.
The Militiaman's God is RIOT.
The Detective's God is PERJUURY.
The Sucker's God is "DE BOSS."
The Scissorbill's God is "MY (?) JOB."
The "Labor Leader's" God is the PIE COUNTER.
The Editor's God is CIRCULATION.
The Hobo's God is REBELLION.
And, the Worker's God is FREEDOM.

---

25   *The Voice of the People*, Vol. III No. 26 (June 30th, 1914).

THE BEARERS OF THE LIGHT[26]
Henry M. Tichenor

What though you sawed Isaiah in the hollow of a tree,
What though you hung the Nazarene upon Mount Calvary,
What though the Sage of Athens did the poison hemlock take,
What though your vile religion burned great Bruno at the stake—
What though a million martyred ones have gone your bloody way,
Their souls, ye wolves, you could not kill, they're with us all to-day!

You think that now you'll hide your guilt beneath a saintly sham—
For all your philanthropic gifts we do not give a damn!
Your libraries and colleges, endowments great and small,
Your churches and cathedrals, we spurn them one and all!
Your monster creeds and humbugs, your goblins and your hell,
No longer on our quickened brains conjure their magic spell!

Go—take them where you forged them, back to the savage night—
we follow those you thought were dead, the Bearers of the Light!

HEAR![27]
Omar

O Thou, who didst with Pitfall and with Gin
Beset the Road I was to wanter in;
Thou wilt not with Predestination round
Enmesh me, and impute my Fall to Sin?

O Thou, who Man of baser Earth didst make
And who with Eden didst devise the Snake;
For all the Sin wherewith the Face of man
Is blacken'd Men's Forgiveness give—and TAKE!

---

26   *The Voice of the People*, Vol. II No. 31 (August 7th, 1913). Source notes this was reprinted from *The Melting Pot*.
27   *The Voice of the People*, Vol. II No. 30 (July 31st, 1913).

A PRAYER TO LUCIFER[28]

God of Light Bearers, known of old,
God of the Rebels, free and bold,
Sound fourth thy trumpet! Let us hear
Its silver notes ring far and clear!

In this stricken, slave-cursed world,
Let now thy thunderbolts be hurled;
In freedom's name, for truth and right,
God of my fathers, hurl the light!

Send out once more thy clarion call,
"Life to the brave! Death to the thrall!"
God of the Rebels, lead thine own,—
Behold the Bond Lord on thy throne!

Breathe on them thy mighty breath;
To mutiny stir the doomed to death;
To revolution or their graves,
God of my fathers, call his slaves!

From liberty's unconquered halls,
From out their grand and rugged wlls,
In freedom's name, for truth and right,
God of the Rebels, hurl the light!

---

[28] *The One Big Union Monthly,* Vol. 3 No. 4 (April 1938).

ONWARD CHRISTIAN SOLDIERS[29]
Wm. Lloyd Garrison

The Anglo Saxon Christians, with gatling gun and sword
In serried ranks are pushing on the gospel of the Lord;
On Afric's soil they press the foe in war's terrific scenes
And merrily the hunt goes on throughout the Philippines.

What though the Boers are Christians; the Filipinos, too!
It is a Christian act to shoot a fellow creature through.
The bombs with dynamite surcharged their deadly missiles fling,
And gaily on their fatal work the dum-dum bullets sind.

The mahdis and the sirdars along the great Soudan
Are learning at the cannon's mouth the brotherhood of man;
The holy spirit guides aloft the shrieking shot and shell,
And Christian people shout with joy at thousands blown to hell.

The pulpits bless the victor and praise the bloody work,
As after an Armenian raid rejoiced the pious Turk;
The Christian press applauds the use of bayonet and knife,
For how can social order last without the strenuous life?

The outworn, threadbare precept, to life the poor and weak,
The fallacy that this great earth is for the saintly meek;
Have both gone out of fashion: the world is for the strong;
That might be the lord of right is now the Christian song.

Then onward Christian soldier, though the fields of crimson gore,
Behold the trade advantages beyond the open door!

---

29 *The Voice of the People*, Vol. II No. 30 (July 31st, 1913). Source notes this was reprinted from *The Melting Pot*.

THE HONEST BURGLAR[30]
Rev. M. A. Smith

The banker calls it "interest,"
    And heaves a pious sigh.
The landlord calls it "rent,"
    And he winks the other eye.
The merchant calls it "profit,"
    And he tucks it in the bag.
But the good old honest burglar,
    He simply calls it "swag."

A CONJURATION[31]
Dedicated to the "Higher Thoughts."
Voc The Barbarian

The sun is but the tail-end of a monstrous fire-fly,
The moon is but a big glow-worm acrawlin' 'cros the sky;
The comets they ain't nothin', sir, but gasbags ful o' wind,
Just iridescent hotair by the seraph statesmen spinned.

The things they call the planets, an' the things they calls the stars,
Aint nothin', sir, but cat's eyes aglowin' from afars;
The earth's a hollow bubble, just a soapskin 'round a hole,
An' full o' creepin' microbes what believes they is a soul.

The whole of all creation is the shadder of a dream,
The ghostly conjuration, sir, of things that only seem,
An' its a fact past doubtin', which can never be gainsed,
We's never really livin' an' we's never really dead.

---

30   *The Voice of the People,* Vol. II No. 34 (August 28th, 1913). Source notes this was reprinted from *The Rebel.*
31   *The Voice of the People,* Vol. II No. 45 (November 13th, 1913).

FAILURE[32]
(To the failures of the world who
alone have known the cost of failure.)

I gazed into the face of Failure; felt her hunger-stricken eyes
Burn deep into my bosom, and I heard her low, despairing cries;
I felt her cold arms folding 'round me, like the cold arms of the dead,
And all my strength was numbed and broken, and my heart was
 turned to lead.

I heard her wildly calling, urging on the wolves of Grief and Hate;
I saw her slaves unleashing all the terrors in the house of Fate;
I heard her hyena, Fear, shrieking on life's dark and barren plain.
And felt the throb of madness sweep like fire through my soul and brain.

I saw Love's gardens blasted by a sudden, icy breath,
And Hope's beloved body quiv'ring in the vulture-clasp of Death;
I saw the golden dreams and visions, I had fought for through the years,
With broken wings plunge headlong in the soundless, dark abyss of tears.

I saw the awful haunts of poverty, where live the living-dead,
And sat down at the tables where gaunt harpies served us stones for
 bread;
I saw myself a kinsman of half human brutes, of men defiled,
Returned to all the loathsome instincts and the passions of the wild.

I gazed into the face of Failure, of the demoness whose reign,
Of heartless, soulless splendor, blights the land where Mercy lieth slain;
And all that ever was of sorrow it was deeply written there,
And there I read the piteous story of soul-hunger and despair.

---

[32] *The Voice of the People,* Vol. 2 No 36 (September 11, 1913).

A NIGHTMARE'S NEST

(Dedicated to the American
Revolutionary Labor Movement.)

Voc, The Barbarian

"Race me a race," the race horse said;
"Hop me a hop" said the hoppergrass;
"You're juney and bugs," said the bug;
And, "You talk like an ass," said the ass.
"Quick! flip me a flop," said the flea;
"No! shoo me a shoofly," said the fly;
"Cease! cease!" said the worm, "ere I turn!"
"Ay!" the goggle-eye said, "in my eye!"
"Indite me a bull," said the bull;
"Wail me a waul," said the cata-wall;
"O rats!" said the rat, "you are bats!"
"Nay, rattled!" said the bat, "that is all!"
Yea! Yea! 'tis the truth that I tell,
They were foozled and fumbled and fixed;
And all that they said, as I say,
It was bumbled and jumbled and mixed!"

WHAT LUCIFER WROTE

Kaufman

"Why! as I live—there's a tear in his eye,
Now what in hell can make Lucifer cry?
Surely the rebel is feeling his age—
Look what he's writing on Isabel's page;
'Virtue is a luxury hard to afford
When a girl hasn't money enough for her board.'"

---

33   *The Voice of the People*, Vol. II No. 37 (September 18th, 1913).
34   *The Voice of the People*, Vol. II No. 49 (December 11th, 1913).

YE "RESPECTABLES"[35]

Ye leprous "saints" who criticise the "erring brother's way,"
Who never yet with Naked Hands have held the Fates at bay;
How Dare ye sit in judgement on the Soul at last o'erthrown,
Ye craven curs who never Dared to face the Dark alone?

Hark! Back there in the Ages, out in every Land and Clime,
I hear your Wolfish barking there, on every road of Time;
I hear your hissing laughter when your Quarry down is run,
As ye laughed upon Golgotha when your hellish work is done.

In smug, fat-bellied splendor, safe, in Customs mantle wrapt,
Ye hurled *your* God's damnation and the blood of Heroes lapt—
Ye never heard from Virtue and ye never spoke with Love,
Else ye would not try to fright us with Your image throned above.

The changing of Religions has not ever changed your Creed—
Through all the stricken ages ye have bred true to your Breed—
The Faith ye preach so loudly is your deathless faith in Pelf—
Your God is but the image of your own time-serving Self.

Besides the graves of Freedom, there your vulture wings are flapt,
And we heard your joyous croaking when the forts of Right were sapt;
Man never yet have seen ye in the forefront of the Line,
Where the shells of truth are screaming and the swords of Justice shine.

As ye were in all past ages, So ye are down to to-day—
Beloved of all the Priesthoods—quick to murder as to pray—
Sleek vampires, full to bursting with the Pure Blood of the Right—
Ye Werewolves of the Darkness and ye Ghoulhounds of the Night!

---

35   *The Voice of the People*, Vol. III No. 9 (February 26th, 1914).

I, THE KEPT PRESS[36]

I am the Kept Press—
Belial, god of lust and degeneracy,
Was my father—
A crocodile without tears,
Was my mother—
I am a human ghoul ravaging an earth-wide Golgotha
The putrid ghost of Plutocracy raving thru a wilderness
    of graves—
An intellectual hireling—
Without honor, shame or conscience—
And proud of it!—
Woe to the Truth Speakers!—
Death to the Light Bearers!—
Long live the Liberticides!

OUR BOY-HEART[37]

Voc, The Barbarian

It died so hard, our boy-heart! And it fought the dark so long!
So long it held the vision and so long it heard the song!
It would not quit the battle till the rout was all complete,
And dreamland's splendid armies were in slow and sad retreat.

Up in our faces smiling, long it held, the world at bay
And threw hope's glowing rainbows on life's shadows dim and gray;
Up in our faces smiling, through the mysts it led us on.
Through myst and storm and midnight in the long search for the dawn.

Up in our faces smiling, till the dark was all supreme,
The music hushed forever and the death-hand on the dream;
Up in our faces, smiling, with the sunny faith of old,
Our boy-heart died in battle in the Gardens of the Soul.

---

36   *The One Big Union Monthly*, Vol. 1 No. 8 (October 1919).
37   *The Voice of the People*, Vol. III No. 13 (March 26th, 1914).

PEOPLE WILL TALK[38]
(Unsigned)

You may get through the world, but 'twill be very slow,
If you listen to all that is said as you go;
You'll be worried and fretted, and kept in a stew—
For meddlesome tongues must have something to do,
    And people will talk.

If quiet and modest, you'll have it presumed
That your humble position is only assumed—
You're a wolf in sheep's clothing, or else you're a fool,
But don't get excited—keep perfectly cool—
    For people will talk.

And then, if you show the least boldness of heart,
Or slight inclination to take your own part,
They will call you an upstart, conceited and vain,
But keep straight ahead—don't stop to explain—
    For people will talk.

If threadbare your dress, or old-fashioned your hat,
Some one will surely take notice of that,
And hint rather strong that you can't pay your way,
But don't get excited, whatever they say—
    For people will talk.

If you dress in the fashion don't think to escape,
For they criticise then in a different shape;
You're ahead of your means, or your tailor's unpaid,
But mind your own business—there's naught to be made—
    For people will talk.

Now, the best way to do is to do as you please;
For your mind, if you have one, will then be at ease.
Of course, you will meet with all sorts abuse;
But don't think to stop them—it ain't any use—
    For people will talk.

---

[38] *The Voice of the People*, Vol. III No. 30 (August 6th, 1914).

WAR[39]
Adolf Wolff

Behold the minions of "Law and Order."
The guardian angels of "Property and Life."
Behold their blood-drenched standards waving
In breezes pestilential, sowing death,
Disease, despair and devastation.
Behold their priests implore their helpless gods
To grand their arms omnipotence in murder.

Oh, will those who survive this mighty carnage
At last perceive that all these cursed rulers
Stand only for the LAW of death
And the ORDER of destruction?

MIGHT IS RIGHT[40]

Might is Right when Long-Bell builds
A hell 'round every earth;
Might is Right when Kirby starves
His peons off the earth;
And Might was Right when Deitz Became
Wolfe Weyerhauser's prey—
'Tis the logic of the Ancient World,
And the Gospel of Today.

Might is Right when children die
By the thousands in the mills,
When jeweled hands reach down and take
The gold their blood distills;
And Might is Right when maidens give
Their love-dreams up for pay—
'Tis the logic of the Ancient World,
And the Gospel of Today.

And, so, O Hosts of Toil, awaken!
O workingmen, unite!
And by the Might of Folded Arms,
In GENERAL STRIKE sweep 'way,
The fang-law of the Ancient World,
The Gospel of Today!

---

39   *The Voice of the People*, Vol. II No. 34 (September 3rd, 1914). Source notes this was reprinted from *Mother Earth*.
40   This variant from *The Lumberjack* Vol. 1. No. 10. March 13, 1913.

OUR PRIMER OF CELEBRITIES[41]
(Unsigned)

See the War Lord.

Yes, you have guessed it truly. He is a king by divine right. This must be so, because he says it himself. And he knows.

What does the War Lord do?

Oh, many things. For instance, he talks of peace between wars while he is getting ready to fight.

Dear, dear! Does he love to fight?

Well, yes, in a way. But he doesn't like to fight unless it is for honor, or principle or something like that.

Then he loves to fight and kill as many as he can. And when it is all over and his honor has been vindicated, all the widows and orphans are so glad.

Isn't that strange? Tell me; are there many war lords left?

Not many. And there won't be any after a while.

You don't say! When will that time be?

Pretty soon—pretty soon—unless all signs fail.

OFFENSIVE NEATNESS[42]
(Flies try to he clean; they wipe their feet frequently.—Scientific Note.)

Flies may be neat and wipe their feet;
    I will admit all that.
They also take your pie or cake
    And use it as a mat.

These pesky pests, unbidden guests,
    In wiping their soiled soles,
Can't use the floor; they much prefer
    Your flaky breakfast rolls.

The tribe of flies, it really tries,
    It seems, to give offense.
It is not meet to be so neat.
    At other folks' expense.

---

41   *The Voice of the People*, Vol. II No. 39 (October 15th, 1914). Source notes this was reprinted from *Life*.

42   *The Voice of the People*, Vol. II No. 43 (November 12th, 1914).

HOW MUCH CAME TRUE?[43]
Wilby Heard

To you who have toiled since your childhood day,
And visioned sweet dreams in the far away,
And hoped that your labor so earnestly sowed
Would yield in your noontide a rich harvest load;
You figured returns as all planters do—
Now tell me, how much of it ever came true?

You dreamed as you toiled of the sweet scented wood
Of the warbling bird and the dove that cooed,
You longed for the streams and flowers aglow,
And the skies of blue with their clouds of snow,
You longed to enjoy them as all children do—
Now tell me, how much of it ever came true?

And then as you waned into later years,
You could have vowed you'd avoid bitter tears,
You felt in your bones love's blossoming force;
Planned to sail smooth o'er its life filling course,
New dreams then awoke as Love's visions do—
Now tell me, how much of it ever came true!

You labored and trusted, faithfully prayed
The God of your sires beseeching his aid.
You gave to your master your brain and your hand
In hope that some day together you'd stand,
But you drifted apart, all opposites do—
Now tell me, how much of your prayers came true?

You labored and thirsted, hungered and sought,
While your masters did maw all that you wrought.
Your God never answered pleading proved vain,
The thieves have the riches you have the chain.
But still you slave on as all good slaves do—
Now tell me, you wage slave, say, isn't this true?

The forest, the bird, the dove and the streams,
The flowers, the skies, and the clouds of your dreams,
The love of your youth, and the visions it bore
Are still within reach, and waiting in store
For those who'll rebel, who'll dare and who'll do—
Just try it you toiler, you'll find this is TRUE.

---

[43] *The Voice of the People*, Vol. II No. 42 (November 5th, 1914).

THE HOBO'S BOAST[44]

I am the bondless spirit all the race must recognize!
In me the soul of labor still stands free beneath the skies;
In me the soul of Freedom, still unconquered, marches on—
I am the hope of liberty—the herald of the dawn!

I am the hope of liberty, earth's Lucifer today;
The dread within the heart of kings, the sword within their way;
The block on which their heads shall fall, the knife that shears them off;
I am the great avenger, I! the "thing" at which they scoff.

I am the hope of liberty—its star is in my hand;
By me its light is scattered thru the dark of every land;
By me Wrong's mask is shattered and the veil of Custom rent—
I spread thru all the cities far the flames of discontent.

I am the bondless spirit all the race must recognize!
In me the soul of Labor still stands free beneath the skies;
In me the soul of Freedom, still unconquered, marches on—
I am the hope of liberty—the herald of the dawn!

FODDER FOR CANNON[45]
Katharine Lee Bates

Bodies glad, erect,
Beautiful with youth,
Life's elect,
Nature's truth,
Marching host on host,
Those bright, unblemished ones,
Manhood's boast,
Feed them to the guns.

Hearts and brains that teem
With blessing for the race,
Thought and dream,
Vision, grace,
Oh, love's best and most,
Bridegrooms, brothers, sons,
Host on host
Feed them to the guns.

---

44 *Rebellion* Vol. 1 No. 12 (June 1916).
45 *The Voice of the People,* Vol. II No. 41 (October 29th, 1914). Source notes this was reprinted from *Life*.

A REBEL'S DREAM[46]
Cash M. Stevens

My dreams are not of the present time,
Nor songs that bards have sung;
They are not of a race of servile slaves
Who will not defend their young

But I dream tonight of the olden time,
Of the ancient long ago;
And my spirit flies on fancy's wings
To the days of spear and bow.

The lives I have lived and the deaths I have died,
Seem to linger in memory still;
For I rode in the ranks of the Rebel Clan,
That turned no master's mill.

I lived and died as I'll die again,
With the blood red Rebel Clan;
That laughs to scorn both priests and kings,
And the cob-web laws of man.

I'll fight to the end all gold-made law,
That has made this earth a hell;
I'll fight as I fought in San Antonio,
On the day the Alamo fell.

I have fought and died in the rebel ranks,
I have bled for the toiling slaves;
I have shared their lives, I have died their deaths,
I have shared their lonely graves.

But the call of the Clan is sounding loud,
O'er valley and hill and plain—
Will you stand as of old in the rebel ranks,
And fight to be free again?

The ages come and the ages go,
And death must follow the van;
When he comes again he will find me still,
In the ranks of the Rebel Clan.

---

[46] *The Voice of the People*, Vol. III No. 5 (January 29th, 1914).

THE CURIOUS CHRISTIANS[47]
A Heathen

For "Jesus' sake" they shoot you dead,
They fill you full of steel and lead;
They wreck your body, crush your soul,
They pray to God to "make you whole."

They stand for war—with fervent breath
They bless the instruments of death;
They flap the flag, they shout for blood,
Then weep beside the crimson flood.

They strike the light from woman's eyes,
Then "charitably" hush her cries;
They slay her husband, take her child,
Then tract her on "love undefiled."

They say, "'Tis not by bread alone
That mankind cometh to its own;"
Then strive to bind the spirit's wings.
The upward sweep of changing things.

They preach "good will" and "peace" and "love,"
"The golden rule," all else above;
They teach the brotherhood of man as true.
Then turn their war-dogs loose on you.

Ah, verily, they say and say.
And preach and preach and pray and pray;
Yet still the harvest comes as sown.
Still by its fruit the tree is known.

---

47   *Rebellion* Vol. 1 No. 3 (May 1915). Reprinted in *The New Magazine*, a suppliment of *The Daily Worker* (Dec. 18, 1926) and attributed to Covami under the title, and then "covington Hall, Mena, Ark." at the end. It has been included in modern poetry anthologies *You Work Tomorrow: An Anthology of American Labor Poetry, 1929-41* and *Repression and Recovery: Modern American Poetry and the Politics of Cultural Memory 1910-1945.*

A HYMN TO HATE[48]

O thou, twin-born with Love from Beauty's line,
Her alter ego and, like her, divine!
To thee I lift my voice in feeble praise!
To thee, admiring, my eyes I raise!
To thee whose fructifying kiss, O Hate,
So oft hath 'couraged men to challenge fate!

Thou art not evil-thou are good and fair!
To thee we owe the strength of our despair;
To thee alone, when all around is night,
When Hope is dead and Love herself in flight—
To thee we owe the iron strength and will
To battle for emancipation still.

'Tis not till slavery's hated by the slaves—
'Tis only then Truth rises from her graves—
'Tis only then that Freedom comes to birth—
'Tis only then Love glorifies the Earth—
'Tis only then, O Hate, 'tis only then—
After thou hast cleansed the hearts of men!

It is because Toil's legions know thee not,
Theirs is the burden's brunt, the bitter lot;
Theirs is the robot task, the servile name,
The tenant's rags, the peon's wage and shame:
Because of this, O Hate, because of this—
They have not felt thy fructifying kiss!

THE PROPHET'S CURSE[49]

The Prophet-soul can never rest:
It cannot see, What is, the best;
By a strange demon 'tis possest—
It has a conscience in its breast.

---

48 *The New Magazine: Supplement of The Daily Worker* (November 27, 1926).
49 *The One Big Union Monthly* New Series Vol. 2 No. 1 (January 1938).

CONFESSIONS[50]

I admit it—
I prefer—
Lucifer to Jehova—

Astarte to Minerva—
Widows to Virgins—
Sinners to Saints—
Reds to Respectables—
Hoboes to Heroes—
"Niggers" to "Supreme Whites"—
And—
Rattlesnakes to Reformers—
The first are All so Much More Interesting—
Put so much more Pep into life—
And—
While they are at it—
Don't care a damn—
Whether or No—
"Business as Usual"—
goes to hellornot.—
Same here.

I admit it—
I Don't admire—
He-Men—
She-Women—
Soul-Kissers—
"Captains of Industry"—
"Labor Leaders"—
"Wizards of Finance"—
Dime Distributors—
Patriots—
Pollywogs—
And—
Progressifs—
They give me a pain—
They are All so Dull and Dumb—
Damn Respectability, anyhow.

---

50   From *The Industrial Worker* (Dec. 28, 1929).

O GLOWING LAND OF DIXIE[51]

O glowing Land of Dixie, crowned with blue-gray mountain domes,
You were made for noble women, you were made for freemen's homes;
For a breed as strong and upstanding as the Arab, and as bold
As ever were the Indians and the Grecian tribes of old.

The light that falls upon your streams was never made to bless
The hearthstones of the servile, who the rights of Lords confess;
Not for tenants and peons was your clean, warm bosom made,
And not for the degenerate your sunshine and your shade.

Your very air is vital with the essences of life,
The haunting mists that veil you with eternal beauty rife;
And so, I dream, O Dixie, that, with souls no longer dumb,
From out your plains and forests yet a conq'ring breed shall come.

A breed that will not falter, nor from justice turn aside,
Nor lose to greed its honor will the last of them has died;
A breed of lofty purpose, free, without a king or slave,
The master of its destiny, as upright as 'tis brave.

THE STRIKE[52]

Say what ye will, ye owls of night,
The strike upholds the cause of right;
The strike compels the king to pause,
The statesmen to remould the laws.

Say what ye will, yet, without ruth,
The strike drives home the bitter truth;
The strike tears off the mask of things,
To mass and class the issue brings.

Say what ye will, the strike is good—
It clears things long misunderstood;
It jolts the social mind awake;
It forces men a stand to take.

Say what ye will, all else above,
The strike is war for bread and love;
For raiment, shelter, freedom, all
The human race can justice call.

---

51 *The Press and Standard* (Walterboro, South Carolina) (Jul 25, 1946). Printed in *Batle Hymns of Toil*.
52 *The Voice of the People*, Vol. II No. 28 (July 17th, 1913).

THE SONS OF THE SERPENT[53]

The Sons of the Serpent are the Sons of the Light,
And the Sons of the Serpent are the Heroes of Might;
'Twas a Son of the Serpent who learned us of Life
And sent us Wisdom's message through our father Adam's wife.

The Sons of the Serpent are the leaders, the van,
Are the agents of Lucifer, the teachers of Man;
They acknowledge no Caesar over earth, sky or sea,
So the Sons of the Serpent have forever been free.

A PRAYER TO THOR[54]

"God of our fathers, known of old,"
God of the Northmen, free and bold,
Sound forth thy trumpet; let us hear
Its silver notes ring far and clear!

Into this slave-cursed, stricken world,
Let now thy thunderbolts be hurled;
In freedom's name, for truth and right,
God of our fathers, hurl the light!

Send out once more thy clarion call,
"Life to the Brave, death to the Thrall!"
God of our fathers, lead thy own—
Behold the Bond Lord on thy throne!

Breathe on them thy mighty breath;
To mutiny stir the doomed to death;
To Revolution or their graves,
God of our fathers, call his slaves!

From free Valhalla's splendid halls,
From out its grand and rugged walls.
In freedom's name, for truth and right,
God of our fathers, send the light!

---

53 *The Voice of the People*, Vol. III No. 10 (March 5th, 1914).
54 *Rebellion* Vol. 1 No. 12 (June 1916). The first line is quoting the first line of the poem "Recessional" (1897) by Rudyard Kipling.

Bibliography
(CHRONOLOGICAL)

JOURNAL EDITOR
The Lumberjack Vol.1 No. 1, January 9, 1913 – Vol. 1 No. 27, July 10, 1913
The Voice of the People Vol. 2 No. 28 1913 – Vol. 2 No. 51, December 25th, 1914
Rebellion: Made up of Dreams and Dynamite Vol. 1. No. 1, March 1915 – Vol. 1 No. 12, June 1916.
The Vanguard, New Llano, LA, 1924 (This was a paper founded by Kate Richards O'Hare and moved to New Llano in 1923)
Industrial Democrat, 1931-'32 (He would return as a "contributing editor" in 1934-'35)

BOOKS
Songs of Love and Rebellion (New Orleans: John J. Weihing Printing Co., 1915)
Rhymes of Rebel (New Llano: Llano Co-operative Colony Printery, 1931)
Quivara, or The Quest of Alvarez (Rogers: Avalon Press, 1946)
Battle Hymns of Toil (Oklahoma City: General Welfare Reporter, 1946)
Dreams & Dynamite: Selected Poems, edited by Dave T. Roediger (Chicago: Charles H. Kerr Publishing Company, 1985)
Labor Struggles in the Deep South (Chicago: Charles H. Kerr Publishing Company, 1999)
Covington Hall's Satanic Lumberjacks and Southron Rebels, edited by Kevin I. Slaughter (Baltimore: Union of Egoists, 2019)

OTHER
American Life Histories: Manuscripts from the Federal Writers' Project, 1936 to 1940; Alabama Writers' Project.; Federal Writers' Project:
Folder 28: Hall, Covington (interviewer): The Andrew Jackson of Southern Labor
Folder 29: Hall, Covington (interviewer): Mountain Thinker and Experimenter
Folder 30: Hall, Covington (interviewer): Mountain Merchant-Farmer
Folder 31: Hall, Covington (interviewer): Sam Cash, Farmer-Miner

GHOST TITLE
The Lodestar New Orleans, LA. This publication was announced in *Strike Bulletin* (Clinton, Ill.), January 20, 1915 and also *The International Socialist Review*, March 1915. It is unclear how many, if any, issues were published. In 1925 Commonwealth Labor College started a newspaper. Two issues in the first year, Vol. 1 Nos. 10-11, were titled *The Lodestar*. Covington Hall was a teacher at the college on and off. It is unclear if there is any connection.

STANDARD FREETHOUGHT WORKS

A SECRET HIT: 150 YEARS OF...*DER EINZIGE*...—Bernd Laska $9
CONFESSIONS OF A FAILED EGOIST—*Trevor Blake*. $10
ELBERT HUBBARD'S THE PHILISTINE—*Bruce A. White* $16
HOMO 99 AND $^{44}/_{100}$ NONSAPIENS—*Gerald B. Lorentz*. $18
MIGHT IS RIGHT: THE AUTHORITATIVE EDITION—*Ragnar Redbeard* $20
MIGHT IS RIGHT: 1927 FACSIMILE EDITION—*Ragnar Redbeard* $16
THE OCCULT TECHNOLOGY OF POWER—*The Transcriber*. $8
THE PHILOSOPHICAL WRITINGS OF EDGAR SALTUS—*Edgar Saltus* $18
THE RADICAL BOOK SHOP OF CHICAGO—*Kevin I. Slaughter* $15
THE RED SECT—*Enzo Martucci*. $15
RIVAL CAESARS: A ROMANCE...—*Ragnar Redbeard* $20
THE SATANIC SCRIPTURES—*Peter H. Gilmore*. $17
SORCERIES AND SCANDALS OF SATAN—*Henry M. Tichenor* $15
THIS UGLY CIVILIZATION—*Ralph Borsodi*. $20

BENJAMIN DeCASSERES SERIES:
ANATHEMA! LITANIES OF NEGATION $10
FANTASIA IMPROMPTU & FINIS $16
FULMINATIONS: CAUSTIC, COSMIC, CAPRICIOUS $16
IMP: THE POETRY OF BENJAMIN DeCASSERES $15
NEW YORK IS HELL: THINKING AND DRINKING IN THE BEAUTIFUL BEAST . . $18
SPINOZA: LIBERATOR OF GOD AND MAN & AGAINST THE RABBIS $15
THE BOY OF BETHLEHEM—Bio DeCasseres (Hardbound) $23
THE SUBLIME BOY—*Walter DeCasseres*. $7

THE PORTABLE L.A. ROLLINS SERIES:
THE MYTH OF NATURAL RIGHTS $15
LUCIFER'S LEXICON $15
OUTLAW HISTORY $15
DISJECTA MEMBRA . . . . (coming soon)

PAMPHLETS

BOVARYSM: THE ART-PHILOSOPHY OF JULES DE GAULTIER—*Wilmot E. Ellis* . . $4
IMMORALITY AS A PHILOSOPHIC PRINCIPLE—*Paul Carus* $5
MAX STIRNER AND THE PHILOSOPHY OF THE INDIVIDUAL—*Leo Markun* . . . $8
MAN-EATING AND MAN-SACRIFICING—*Anon*. $3
THE NIETZSCHE MOVEMENT IN ENGLAND—*Oscar Levy* $2
PRIMITIVES: POEMS AND WOODCUTS—*Max Weber* $6
TUMBSCREW AND RACK—*Geo. B. Macdonald*. . . . . (coming soon)

UNDERWORLD AMUSEMENTS
444 MARYLAND AVE. #7940   ESSEX, MD 21221
Add $4 for the first item, $1 for each additional for postage.
Or visit WWW.UNDERWORLDAMUSEMENTS.COM

www.ingramcontent.com/pod-product-compliance
Lightning Source LLC
Chambersburg PA
CBHW052128070526
44586CB00016B/2136